Poems Between Here and Beyond

by
David L. Hatton

Cover Image:
"The Stages of Life" (1835, cropped)
by Caspar David Friedrich (1774-1840)

This book is available for the Kindle Reader from
amazon.com
✻ ✻ ✻ ✻ ✻ ✻
Single copies of many of these poems are downloadable as PDF files for printing and sharing with others from the "Poetry" page on **pastordavidrn.com**.

Copyright © 2016 David L. Hatton
All rights reserved.
ISBN-13: 978-1535440479
ISBN-10: 1535440473

DEDICATION

To the classic poets of the past,

who taught me as a child to love good poetry,
and whose timeless examples have always kept me
desirous to improve my own poetic skills.

by David L. Hatton

TABLE OF CONTENTS

INTRODUCTION	7
IN BETWEEN	11
IMBECILITY	12
AFTERLIFE	12
BEGINNING WISDOM	13
BLESSINGS	13
THE WIND OF GOD	13
PROTESTERS	14
MY DREAM OCEAN	14
THANKS SO MUCH!	15
SEX VOW	16
CHRIST IS FIRST	16
SUPERSTITION	17
ROSEMARY	18
REDEEMING DEADLY SINS	18
BREVITY	18
CALLINGS	19
WRITE!	19
BE OF GOOD CHEER	20
CONFESSION	21
NOW AND THEN	22
WEDDED GRATITUDE	23
MOM AND DAD'S 30TH ANNIVERSARY	23
FARTHER ON	24
CAUTION	24
LIFE'S TRAIN	25
PLEASANTRIES AFTER MIDNIGHT	26
THE DEAD	26
CLOUDS	27
SOUND ADVICE	28
PART OF THE CROWD	28
NO GRAY IN GOD	30

PLAGIARISTS	31
SOLID	31
EASTER HOPE	32
A SHORT TRIP	32
CREATORS	33
WORD PLAY	34
THE INCARNATE GOD	34
ADELPHOR AND MORE	35
BODY LANGUAGE	39
BABIES	40
EQUATIONS	41
EVERLASTING	42
PREVENIENT GRACE	43
GRIEF	44
CHOSEN	45
DEFENDING HEAVEN AND HELL	45
PUNCTUATION'S ERADICATION	46
THE DISCUS THROWER	49
MY MARRIED HEART	49
QUESTIONS	50
WHAT LASTS	51
THE LOVE OF GOD	52
VENGEANCE	53
GLORY	54
TERMINUS	55
GENDER	56
INQUISITION	57
ETERNITY	58
SOUL SLEEP	59
MY SISTER, MY SPOUSE	60
EDEN'S TABLE	60
ORIGINAL SKIN	62
OLD WEBS	62
TEARS OF LOSS	63
WHEN PRIDE IS BROKEN	64

THE BODY SPEAKS	64
WORTH REPEATING	66
JUDGMENT	67
REMINISCENCES	68
RETIRING FROM NURSING	69
COUNTING DELIVERIES	70
REUNION	71
ONE FAMILY	71
EVER-CIRCLING YEARS	72
CAN I ONLY GUESS?	73
MATERNAL POWER	74
CARING	75
MENTAL FOG	75
DOOM	76
GHOST OF A CHANCE	76
A SADDLED HORSE	78
JUST BECAUSE	79
LOVE THAT LASTS	80
GREEN DOLPHIN STREET – 1947	81
THE WILL	82
DISILLUSIONMENT	83
CELLS	84
COMMUNITY	84
WISDOM	85
AUTUMN	86
LE JOUR QUE J'AI NAGÉ NU	86
OMG, GMO!	87
SKINNY-DIPPING	89
MY BEST FRIEND	89
THE WIPING CLOTH	89
GOD CONDEMNED	90
SKEPTICS	91
NATURE'S TOUCH	92
DOMINION	93
SIN'S DOUBLY CAUSTIC	93

GRIEF'S RIPPLES	94
THAT UNBLINDING LIGHT	94
OVERDUE PUN	95
SHAKESPEARE'S PEN	96
HEALP!	97
HOW GOD ANSWERS	97
MOTHER'S DAY	98
DEAD RIVALS	99
PRAYER LIST	99
INDIANA SEASONS	100
BEGINNING GARB	101
THE CHURCH BELL	102
FALSE POETRY	103
HELL'S HARVEST	103
FREE FALL	104
OLD GLORY	105
BREATH OF LIFE	106
GREED	107
WHY SO BIG AND OLD AND DARK?	107
EARTH, EARTH, EARTH	109
FLOWER TALK	110
SEXUAL REMEMBERING	111
"IN REMEMBRANCE OF ME"	112
LABYRINTHINE JOURNEY	113
ABOUT THE AUTHOR	115
INDEX OF TITLES (alphabetical)	117

by David L. Hatton

A lion has roared! Who will not fear?
The Lord GOD has spoken! Who can but prophesy?
— Amos 3:8 (NKJV)

If I read a book and it makes my whole body so cold
no fire can warm me, I know that is poetry.
If I feel physically as if the top of my head were taken off,
I know that is poetry. These are the only ways I know it.
Is there any other way? — Emily Dickinson

My heart is overflowing with a good theme;
I recite my composition concerning the King;
My tongue is the pen of a ready writer.
— Psalm 45:1 (NKJV)

Poems Between Here and Beyond

by David L. Hatton

INTRODUCTION

Ancient Chinese wisdom aptly pictures humans with feet on earth and heads in heaven. We inhabit two worlds, one tangible, measurable, concrete; the other intangible, difficult to measure, often elusive. Men and women are *body-spirit* beings, participating simultaneously in two modes of existence: material and mental. We're not spirits wrapped in flesh or bodies with souls, but a marriage of them, a wedding of the animal and the angelic, an amalgamation of the chemical and the transcendent, a unique union embodying God's image.

We can't escape being replicas of our Creator. If we try denying our God-*likeness*, human art betrays us in paintings, plays, novels, songs, poems and other creative works. We image a Supreme Artist. Or if we try denying God as the Decider of "good and evil," we empty our own personal moralities of meaning. We can't remove an Ultimate Authority from the human equation without forfeiting the divine certainty that we are "very good" parts of creation (Gen 1:31).

Confidence in a Self-revealing God gives us a much more solid and *human-friendly* perspective. His existence (God reveals *Himself* in Scripture as "Father") makes *creativity* and *morality* not just gifts but callings. As image-bearers of the Designer and Judge of all things, we were meant to mimic Him. He calls us to create new designs and to live holy lives.

Communicating truth is also part of that divine image. God is love, and love communicates. So, the God of truth and love is also a Communicator, sharing truth with us and infusing into us a persistent attraction to it. This explains why human creativity is often an attempt to communicate, using story, song, poetry, music, dance, drawing, sculpture.

Perhaps our greatest purpose in imaging God is to be His ruling representatives. He made us mediators, belonging to both the cosmic and celestial worlds. Ultimately, His revealed plan is to bring both realms under a single, divine government administered by human servant-leaders.

This coming reign has a human King, in fact, *"the King of kings and the Lord of lords"* (Rev 19:16). The Old Testament foretold His First Advent—the transcendent God's incarnation into creation as a human being *"to reconcile all things to Himself"* (Col 1:20). The New Testament culminates in His Second Advent: the God-Man's return in His resurrected body to reign over *"a new heaven and a new earth"* (Rev 21:1). Although this renewed universe awaits future fulfillment, it has already begun in the hearts of those following this Savior, Jesus Christ. In a real sense, the future is already here while still on its way.

This *kingdom* context is where I live, think, preach, and write poetry. Along with others in Christ's Body—His Bride, the Church—I serve as one of the King's royal ambassadors in a familiar but foreign land. It's familiar, because He created it, sustains it, and plans to fully renew it. But it's foreign, because human sin and selfishness have misshapen it. His kingdom has come, but it's still coming. Jesus initiated God's salvation plan, but we still pray for His reign's full consummation, using the familiar words He taught us: *"Thy will be done, on earth as it is in heaven"* (Matt 6:10). Christians live in a world of *already* but *not yet*. So does everyone else, even if unconsciously.

As I've aged, I've become more aware of the *body-spirit* nature of humanity. The *here-and-now* of the material world is quite blatant. We spend time and energy maintaining the body and its health, engaging in labor and leisure, accumulating and managing possessions. But the *beyond* of the spiritual world impinges on these material dimensions of life with a long list of immaterial values and virtues, some of which are listed as fruits of the Holy Spirit: *"love, joy, peace, patience, kindness, goodness, faithfulness, gentleness and self-control"* (Gal 5:22-23).

While our spiritual lives anticipate a destiny hereafter, our future afterlife begins here and now. Christ's First Advent

by David L. Hatton

firmly planted the future's presence in historical time. His earthly work established an ongoing beachhead of God's Kingdom in our fallen, sin-scarred world. Tradition calls this holy battalion the *Church Militant*—Christ's loyal followers still engaged in earthly spiritual warfare. The *Church Triumphant* comprises that group of faithful souls who now rest from life's labors, awaiting a reunion with their physical bodies promised by Christ's resurrection. Yet, by that mystery described in the Creed as "the communion of saints," these departed believers are still surrounding us as "*a great cloud of witnesses*" (Heb 12:1), watching our progress in faith and cheering us on to victory. Christians live between a present *here* and future *beyond*.

All my previous poetry books are "*poems between.*" While this introduction explains the name of this fifth one, its title certainly doesn't account for the wide variety of themes and thoughts expressed by the poems included—some written years ago and some included merely for comic relief. But this long preface *does* describe where and in what frame of mind most of them were written. At this stage of my life, I feel even more keenly my location in this "between" mode of living. Yet, although less active now, since my retirement from hospital nursing, I also feel in the midst of dynamic momentum.

We never move through time; time moves through us. Our *present* is without dimension, sandwiched between an irrevocable *past* and an unfurling *future*. The *now* dividing them cannot be subdivided, but it can be wasted. We can ignore our calling as God's image-bearers, squandering the remaining days of our sojourn *between here and beyond* in trivial pursuits. I pray these poems paint pictures, sing songs, preach sermons, tell tales that will stimulate awareness of time's limits and encourage decisions of personal involvement in the present and future reign of the King.

– David L. Hatton

Poems Between Here and Beyond

by David L. Hatton

IN BETWEEN

So, here I stand amid the briny surge
That jostles surf upon the shore,
Review another breaker's jade converge
With bristling foam. My gaze is keen
Upon the far horizon, like a door
That blocks my seeing what's in store,
Fast sealed to hide the future scene. . . .

My feet are barely bathing at the brink
Of possibilities to come,
Yet waves are rolling faster than I think
I ever saw them as a teen
Or in mid-life. My toes feel numb,
As sheets of white to sea succumb,
Recede, no longer to be seen. . . .

No trekking backward trails across the land,
But time to scavenger the beach,
Find shells and shiny treasures in the sand,
Explore the habitat marine,
While creature gems remain in reach. . . .
Still much to learn. . . . God loves to teach,
As I await Him, in between.

– 3/26/2016

IMBECILITY

The written Word
Has passed the night;
In "NOW" unheard
By clouded light.

– 1968

AFTERLIFE

The growth of our dreams
  and our ambitious schemes
To accomplish still more as we age
Are proof, while alive,
  that our souls must survive:
Life on earth only turns the first page. . . .

– 5/24/2013

BEGINNING WISDOM

If you lack Wisdom, humbly ask.
She is a gift that God imparts
With grace to do her holy task
Of forming healthy minds and hearts.

But if you dare to steal His gift,
You pluck and feed upon a curse
That even death may fail to lift–
A fall that grows from bad to worse.

Don't play the role of Satan's fool.
In godly fear, repent of pride.
Be quick to kneel to Heaven's rule,
And you'll find Wisdom at your side.

– 4/4/2013

by David L. Hatton

BLESSINGS

The autumn leaves and leaves of green
Are mixed throughout our earthly scene,
And we of Adam's blood-red race
Are led each day by Heaven's grace
To walk between the old and new
And count up, when the day is through,
The blessings and the gifts of love
That came to us from God above.

– 06/26/2013

THE WIND OF GOD*

God's Wind broods like a mother hen
Over our world, our will, our way,
Our plans, our pains, our quiet pen . . .
With a destiny to obey.

No forcing, no coercion, none—
Just His gentle breeze on our face
To catch, to coax, to call us run
Our Maker's everlasting race.

The passing days will not return,
And wishful thinking often fails.
He blows so that our flames will burn,
But we alone must hoist our sails.

– 5/5/2013

("The wind of God is always blowing,
but you must hoist your sail."* – Fenelon)

PROTESTERS

The snow is falling soft and white;
They scorn its cold and curse its flight.
The breeze is blowing brisk and clean;
Their minds react with thoughts obscene.
Their angry glare through window panes
Stares thanklessly at vibrant rains.
Their ears reject as wretched noise
The songs a nightingale employs.
A weed has flowered in their grass;
Profanity and wrath amass.
A small child gives his toy away;
His parents now restrict his play.
A light and dark-skinned couple walk;
The air is stained with hateful talk.
Protesters voice their ugly sounds,
While beauty's living love abounds.

– 1966 (revised 2016)

MY DREAM OCEAN

Every night . . . some girl:
She is beautiful.
Sometimes I near death
Or do some great feat.
Happiness with her. . . .
I kill biting beasts.
Adventure and fun:
Ancient garb and swords;
Protecting my love.
Pleasantly touching. . . .
My family lost!

by David L. Hatton

My money lost!
My clothing lost!
My homework un-done!
My true love un-won!
Escaping my foe
With slow legs and arms:
Almost being caught.
Kissing and feeling—
"I love you, so much!"
Forms in a jumble,
Loud ringing of bells,
Safe back on land, but
Desire for more ocean.

– 1968

THANKS SO MUCH!
(for the baby clothes)

It's neat when you are new in town
To have a friend like you around.
When I got here I was quite bare,
But you sent something nice to wear!
Now, Momma's milk is sweet, it's true;
She pampers me for pee and poo,
And I have hand-me-downs, you know,
But you gave something great for show!
I'm really grateful for the gift:
Your welcome's given me a lift!
And so, my "THANK YOU" I will send
To let you know you are my friend.

Sincerely, from Amos Bartholomew Hatton
(with some obvious help from his dad)

– 6/1989

SEX VOW

Sacred gift of sex
spent for thrills but meant for wills
solemn vow connects.

– 5/22/2016

CHRIST IS FIRST

Too many times desire fixed my gaze
Upon an object or a lovely face. . . .
This often harmed my soul in subtle ways,
If such attractions stole my heart's first-place.

For I belong to Christ who gave me peace;
My life, with all its length, must be His, too.
If from my lips His praises ever cease,
My first love, owed to Him, would prove untrue.

When I let others enter in-between
My Lord and me, I quickly realize
How spirit-wounded pain is keen,
How vanity can blind my inner eyes.

If led astray by something beautiful,
I've missed the point! All beauty comes from Him!
My adoration is undutiful,
When worldly sparks make holy flames grow dim.

Through poetry, I dare no more embrace
Such petty feelings taking hold of me!
My rhymes must not forget His love and grace,
If I would write my verses faithfully.

– 1/23/1969 (revised 2016)

by David L. Hatton

SUPERSTITION

Reductionists are zealous to defend their faithful stand
That nothing found in nature was divinely wrought or planned.
Because they see no Maker, they deny a Deity,
And trust time, chance, and matter as creation's trinity.
They preach a cosmic universe without a Mind's design,
Where intricate complexities just happen to combine.

But none of them can demonstrate the logic of their creed
That mindless spontaneity made life on earth succeed.
For even their experiments—arranged by mental skill—
Show no sophistication comes at random . . . without will.
Intelligence and thoughtful plans support each test they make
And prove their God-less cosmos an irrational mistake.

"It's obvious," they claim, "the biosphere evolved by chance!"
Such arguments reveal they reason in a circled dance,
Since they have no examples, in the real world that we see,
Of labyrinthine things emerging from simplicity:
No buildings without builders; no machines without a mind;
No products without purpose, that just got here undesigned.

In contrast, their opponents offer instances galore
To show volition's choice behind a daily treasure store
Of items in existence, complicated and complex,
That solely came about because of human intellects.
A billion illustrations—while the skeptics offer none—
Expose the superstitious faith they teach to everyone.

Indeed, it's superstition when a few among the whole
Ignore our human legacy of sensing that each soul
Must answer to a Higher Law, which moral debt describes—
A doctrine not just taught by one but many tongues and tribes.
Since logic, law, and life give stubborn skeptics no relief,
The afterlife alone may have to halt their unbelief.

– 6/7/2013

ROSEMARY

May God's blessing fall on you,
And your faith stay ever true.
May your growth in Christ not cease.
May your walk in Him be peace.
And may all your days be filled
With the purpose He has willed.

– 4/1969

REDEEMING DEADLY SINS

Our avarice denies the Lord
By holding back what it can hoard.
And covetousness wants to own
The world of things its eyes have known.
The endless lust for more, from greed,
Forever takes more than its need.

But generosity befriends
The lonely poor by what it lends.
And gratitude is happy for
The gifts of God within its door.
Contentment looks at all its stuff
And says, "That's more than quite enough!"

–1/16/2009

BREVITY

Verbal brevity is virtue;
Verbosity is vice.
Mouth still flapping after curfew?
Taping should suffice!

– 3/20/2016

by David L. Hatton

CALLINGS

With purpose God leads His dear children along,
Each daughter to duty, each son to a task.
With various verses He teaches one Song
And sings along with us, if only we'll ask.

Though God is the King of all creatures He made,
These callings aren't given by logic or whim
But come through a dance-step that faith has obeyed:
A waltzing of wills, both of us and of Him.

"May I be your Guest and your Guide?" asks the King,
And Heaven descends, if our hearts become host.
But where in the choir He leads us to sing
Is mercy and blessing, not merit and boast.

To till in the garden, to classify beasts
Or govern the world are vocations divine.
No worker fares less than God's prophets and priests:
We dance what our heavenly callings define.

– 12/29/2013

WRITE!

Write
life-line streams—
sunshine beams that glow!
Free their flow, yoke harnessed tight:
steeds in teams will know
driver's dreams. . . .
Write!

– 4/30/2016

BE OF GOOD CHEER
(John 16:33)

Trials and tragedies, trouble and pain,
Hopes that are dashed amid dreams that are slain:
All of these pepper the world where you dwell,
Making your life just a little like hell.

Satan may threaten, and demons may swarm,
Yet I am with you in tempest and storm.
This I will promise: your heart will have peace,
As you let go in My Spirit's release.

Yes, there is darkness, disease and despair
Marring My beautiful world everywhere.
That's why I came, to connect with each loss
By the embrace of My sin-laden Cross.

Be of good cheer in the Message you've heard.
Others have suffered who knew not My Word.
Others are hurting who still know Me not—
Yours is the cross that can light up their lot.

Take tribulations and trials you face . . .
Plunge them in love by the strength of My grace.
Follow My path, when the suffering grows.
Cherish the Cross! It will conquer your foes!

– 7/12/2000 (revised, 1/17/2014)

by David L. Hatton

CONFESSION*

My God, You know my heart and mind,
And You are merciful and kind.
Please, hear Your broken servant speak;
My strength has failed, for I am weak.

O Lord, I loved a damsel fair
With gentle eyes and golden hair,
Who did not walk Your narrow road
Of saving grace and lightened load.

You heard my prayer for her each night
That she might see Your holy light,
To find by it Your joy and peace
And harvest fruit from its increase.

Dear Lord, I tried to think more of
Her soul's conversion than my love.
When telling her this prayerful thought,
I hid my care, but now I'm caught. . . .

My wayward passion is to blame:
I sought her heart and soul the same!
I mixed Your will with my desire;
Forgive me, God, and quench the fire.

O Lord of Mercy, hear my prayer.
Receive her life into Your care.
I yield my wish her heart be mine!
Redeem her soul by Love divine!

– 1967 (revised 4/8/2015)

*(this girl later found Christ and became a lifelong friend)

NOW AND THEN

The monks of old were wise to say,
"Before you take your final breath,
Make it your habit every day
To meditate upon your death."

Those ancient sages weren't morose—
They wanted to prepare the heart,
That whether far away or close,
They'd calmly face their time to part.

Between your NOW that's speeding by
And your forever THEN to come,
God offers gifts before you die,
And you must tally up the sum.

Abundant blessings fill the span
Of life ordained for you to spend,
And finding them is Heaven's plan,
Before you face your journey's end.

So much for you to do and see
Within the number of your days
That you must set priority
Upon pursuing holy ways.

You'll better savor earthly joys
And dearer hold sweet family ties
When undistracted by the toys
You purchase from the worldly wise.

Amid the blossoms in the spring,
And summer sunshine, winter snow,
Rejoice in hearing nature sing,
Until you meet your turn to go.

But know this well, that work and play
Must fall within the limits set
By just how long you get to stay,
If you would leave without regret.

– 2/4/2014

WEDDED GRATITUDE

I'm grateful to the Lord above
That He allowed us two to wed,
To share our lives in growing love
That never dies when we are dead.
I'm thankful that He gave you breath
And intermingled it with mine,
Until we breathe our last in death
Then rise again to drink love's wine.

– 6/22/2013

MOM AND DAD'S
30TH ANNIVERSARY
(sent with a roll of 100 stamps)

Happy Anniversary!
And here's a little treat,
A roll that both of you can taste
That isn't good to eat:
A string of magic carpets
To take you here and there
While you sit back and laugh, or sleep,
Or eat, or wash your hair.

– 12/25/1978

FARTHER ON

Earth's plague of pompous scholars
    ramble to and fro,
So confidently certain
    that they know
The best and final word
    in Science, Faith, and Art.
But all life's knowledge
    is one ray of prismed light;
The finest creeds just anchors
    in a sea of night;
It's after death
    the finest artists' work will start.

– 11/8/2012

CAUTION:
Cigarette smoking may be hazardous to your health.
(from television's old commercials)

Get fine tobacco end to end:
Have a king-size "honk-honk," friend.

There's one that's recessed from the lips;
The new ones all have charcoal chips;
Built into some are springtime trips;
And some are safe(?) with filter tips.

Refreshing coolness you will find
In every mentholated kind.

"I watched him, Mommy, show his stuff.
 The salesman only took one puff."

by David L. Hatton

"Hey, that smells strange; what is its type?"
"Cigar tobacco in a pipe."

"Mine's got the taste worth dying for."
"But mine's quicker with five puffs more."
"I betcha I'll be first to die."
"Yeah, but yours don't satisfy."

"Oh, how I like this new gold pack,
 And taste the richness . . . hack! . . . hack! hack!"
"Coughing problems? Always choking?
 It's too late now, folks, keep on smoking!"

"Hey, pal, before ya leave . . . choke! choke!
 'Ya gotta light? I need a smoke. . . ."

– 1968

LIFE'S TRAIN

Life's train tests believers' integrity
Or registers doubters' passivity,
To sort us all out for eternity.

Terminus is certain; the ride is free;
But what kind of passengers will we be?
Self-guided, or tutored by prophecy?

– 4/11/2016

PLEASANTRIES AFTER MIDNIGHT
(from Eden Hospital E.R. Night Staff)

How sweet it is to come at night,
To work amid the pain and plight,
When with the moments in between
The break room bears a pleasant scene,
There where delectables are sought:
The home-baked goodies Barry brought.

Now we, of those wee-hour folk
(We do not jest, we do not joke),
If it were not for sweets like these
That tickle brain cells, if you please,
How dull of thought and slow of act
We all would be! Now, that's a fact!

As ludicrous as this may seem,
Our hearts and taste buds thank you, Jeanne.
Receive our thanks, we do implore!
But do not stop! Please, send us MORE!!

– 1988

THE DEAD

There's just a layer spread out thin,
Only a fringe of us on earth
Still living here to name the beasts,
Tend the garden and dance with mirth.

Most all of us have flown away
From journeys either short or long
With some yet singing, forced to go
Before they sang a farewell song.

by David L. Hatton

Comparatively few remain
In sun to bask, of fruit to taste,
With tests to take, choices to make,
Led well to work, misled to waste.

Behind are left invested lives—
Once deposited, not returned.
We keep alone the deeds performed,
Decisions chosen, lessons learned.

That huge majority awaits—
Until God's Resurrection Day—
The next sure set of you and me
To feel death take our breath away.

Shall we delight or dread to join
The crowds our souls must greet or grieve?
Our faith in grace or folly's greed
Determines which . . . before we leave.

– 6/27/2015

CLOUDS

You thought such white in skies of blue
    Was only airy stuff—
Soft cotton lightness birds fly through.
    Just insubstantial fluff?
But from that seeming weightless mass
    God showers rain and snow,
Turns hills to sand, makes peaks to pass,
    Borne off in river-flow. . . .

– 3/19/2016

SOUND ADVICE

When you give a talk or speech,
Move lips boldly, without fear!
Put your words in people's reach,
Loud enough for any ear!

When you use your mouth to teach,
Treat your vowels very dear—
Tuck them tightly, I beseech,
Crisp with consonants and clear.

When you're called to stand and preach,
Don't just speak to people near.
If your sermon's meant for each,
Shout so back-pew folks can hear!

– 6/12/2015

PART OF THE CROWD

A pilgrim proclaiming God's warning
Delivered his message with zeal,
But many who gathered were shouting
To drown his rejected appeal.

The hateful horde blasted the prophet,
And many began to grab stones.
In less than a minute his body
Became a red heap of crushed bones.

The unified swell of their yelling
Resounded to Heaven and shook
The throne of the Lord who had sent him,
And He wrote their names in a book.

by David L. Hatton

Soon, one from these brutally banded
Was brought by a stroke in the brain
To stand in the court of the Master
Whose pilgrim their hatred had slain.

"But I never threw a stone at him!"
"Then why was your cheering so loud?
For I heard it merge with his murder,
As you became part of the crowd."

At once, in his mind he relived it:
The drama, the fervor, the thrill
That made him feel one with his neighbors
And right about wishing to kill.

"Shall I condemn you," asked His Maker,
"To carry this blood-guilt alone,
When each had a hand in creating
A mob with a mind of its own?

"The gang bears the blame for its evil—
The mass for its passion so proud.
Your souls shall be sentenced together,
For each gave his will to the crowd."

When sinners or saints, by their folly,
Trade truth for an urge to belong,
They all must face judgment for blending
Their voice with the crimes of the throng.

– 6/5/2014

Poems Between Here and Beyond

NO GRAY IN GOD

The hair of God is never gray
    But always white as snow.
Forever it has been that way—
    It doesn't change or grow.
At least, in visions this is how
I AM indwells eternal Now.

"But why not blond or brown or red
    Of everlasting youth?"
In white all other colors wed
    And demonstrate the truth
That lesser beauties blessing sight
Are prismed from His Triune Light.

There is no gray in God Divine:
    Of shadow, not a hint.
His very Being draws the line,
    Precise and permanent,
To heal our nature's shaded night
By separating dark from bright.

His spoken Word in dazzling beams
    Undims the human heart
Or drives the blind to mental schemes
    For tearing it apart.
No grayness in our choices stand
Before the glow of Heaven's Hand.

Pure whiteness crowning Deity
    Is holiness displayed.
All calls for human piety
    Authentically are made
Straight from the shining Self of One
Whose Light took flesh in Christ, His Son.

— 1/11/2014

by David L. Hatton

PLAGIARISTS

With perceptive eyes wide open,
narrow minds philosophically shut—
totally focused on long-tutored skills,
engrossed in expressing inborn creativity
while oblivious to obvious appropriation—
draftsmen, painters, sculptors, photographers
observe intently and creatively copy
the exquisite display of natural beauty
in nude models, *en plein air* landscapes.

Such artwork may praise the Maker.

But if these meticulous investments,
energized hours of compositional design
are frank, thoughtless, dishonest borrowings—
with the original Artist offered no credit,
which they so furiously demand from others
daring to freely imitate their own works—
then, in their blissfully artistic ignorance,
these creators, in the image of the Creator,
are merely skillful, talented plagiarists.

– 5/11/2016

SOLID

Hammers bang, clang, blast,
crack, pop, drop, clutter workshop;
old anvil stands fast.

– 4/20/2016

EASTER HOPE

Every year, those despairing,
   languishing in the human condition,
   glimpsed a promise of hope
   in the new life of Spring.

Then one year, Hope beckoned
   to a death-bound human race
   from the open mouth
   of an empty tomb.

— 4/16/2016

A SHORT TRIP

I've faithfully tried confessing
My praises for what God gave
On this brief journey of blessing
Conducting me the grave.

When gripes or worrying threw me,
I fought to repel their sway.
If lust or jealousy drew me,
I dared never let them stay.

Yet anger often ignited
At cruelty, evils and wrongs,
Until my heart re-invited
Lost peace back where it belongs.

Regrets were also a bother—
For faults of a moral sort—
But I sent them to my Father,
Who told me, "The trip is short."

by David L. Hatton

Now, as I tally my travels
And treasures of toil and tears,
Time's task of ticking unravels
Trivia's clutter of years.

For not all I did was useful;
My choices, not always right;
Some concepts held were untruthful,
Laid bare in heavenly light.

When sudden cold winds of death blow,
It seems two or three leaves slip—
Reminders, to let us all know
We're on a very short trip.

Life's brevity is a warning,
Instructing us, while alive,
That after we're mourned some morning,
Our souls and deeds will survive.

Be sure, then, to look behind you
At how fast the days have flown.
Shortly, your last one will find you
And harvest the seeds you've sown.

– 4/2/2015

CREATORS

Skilled work we've designed
echos wonders—worlds of art
willed by Maker's Mind.

– 4/23/2016

WORD PLAY

How does this play with phrases
Lure simple sounds to wed
Then loose their fruits of marriage
Inside the reader's head?

What music sets them prancing
To rhythms seen and heard
That captivate our thinking
With syncopated word?

How do they plant a yearning
To watch their dance repeat,
Like paintings we revisit
Or friends we long to greet?

Why does their garden pathway
We haven't strolled for years
Still woo us with its welcome,
Rekindling smiles and tears?

– 5/5/2015

THE INCARNATE GOD

The Second in the Trinity,
Creator of all realms that be,
Stepped into ours, without His might,
Partook of our humanity;
Remaining still the great I AM,
Became that Seed of Abraham
Who'd end the darkness of our night
As both the Lion and the Lamb.

by David L. Hatton

The Lion and the Lamb are one!
Of God and man, the promised Son
Redeemed us from damnation's plight—
From sins that left our souls undone.
By death and empty tomb, our Lord
Brought law and grace into accord
And He, as Way, Truth, Life and Light,
Has human destiny restored.

That cosmic flesh He dared to take
Our King will nevermore forsake
But by its nature shall invite
The Bride to marry Him and make
A wedding royal and divine:
One Flesh enthroned to realign
His ancient plan that would unite
Creation under Adam's line.

– 4/6/2015

ADELPHOR AND MORE

We reached its orbit late November,
Ten galactic quantum leaps,
Departing early in December,
Specimens in storage keeps.

The captain would not log our story—
What we vowed we saw and heard.
He warned us in the laboratory,
"Better not to breathe a word. . . ."

Adelphor was no common planet,
Much like Earth . . . as old, at least.
Our life-scans made us take for granted
It supported plant and beast.

The atmosphere proved so conducive,
Tanks and suits were left behind.
On hover probes, in quests elusive,
Off we sped to search and find.

When I felt drawn to steer toward mountains,
Sally veered to follow too.
On hearing sounds like distant fountains,
Waterfalls came into view.

Before us lay a fertile valley,
Fragrant . . . forested . . . sublime.
Entranced, we slowed, as I and Sally
Grew more spellbound all the time.

At last we met them . . . lovely creatures,
Tinted with flamboyant hues,
With leafy limbs, soft plant-like features,
Naked skin, light greens and blues.

"How charming . . ." quietly I muttered.
"Thank you!" echoed back in kind.
Our ears heard nothing verbal uttered,
Words resounding in our mind.

"May we not also see your beauty?"
Dressed, we felt obscene and rude.
Aware that stripping was our duty,
Soon we stood there, shy and nude.

by David L. Hatton

They grabbed our hands—we were outnumbered—
Heard them laughing, "Let's go swim!"
I thought, 'Unclad and unencumbered,
Wow! Is Sally's body trim!'

As we approached a gentle river,
Flowing through the forest floor,
Her sculptured figure made me quiver:
I'd not seen her so before. . . .

"The Maker means for mates to marry."
"Yes, but she's not mine," I said.
To know my thoughts exposed was scary—
Sally's image filled my head!

Arriving there, I posed a question,
"Where'd you learn to think our words?"
"Within your world, by observation,
Quantum-casting mental birds."

"Why haven't you built ships, to visit?
Minds like yours surpass our own."
"A calling isn't chosen, is it?
We anticipate a Throne."

For hours, we frolicked naked, swimming,
Basking in that paradise.
Until, we heard, with daylight dimming,
Blaring blasts from probe-device.

Though taking samples was our mission,
We surpassed our task by far—
On leaving, made this last petition:
"Tell us, new friends, who you are."

"You haven't guessed? We are but flowers,
Servants . . . students in a school,
Expanding in our Maker's powers,
While awaiting Human rule.

"Investigation of creation,
Finding facts . . . that's your concern.
The Maker, through His Incarnation,
Sought your race at every turn.

"Till He begins that Day of reigning
Over every world that is,
Prepare, as we, without refraining:
Study to be wholly His!"

We hurried back to where we started.
Garments gone! They'd disappeared!
So mounting probes, still bare, we parted.
Back at ship, the crewmen jeered!

The teams they launched next day and after
Failed to find that mountain vale.
Surrounded by their doubts and laughter,
We no longer told our tale.

But during leaves, we often dated,
Finding spots to skinny-dip,
And later left the service, mated,
Blessed by our Adelphor trip.

– 3/7/2016

by David L. Hatton

BODY LANGUAGE

When we have wounds God doesn't heal
And start to doubt His goodness real,
The Lord may have a deeper goal—
To heal disease within the soul.

The illness felt in flesh and bones
Betrays our inner being's groans
That long to see God's grace revealed
And yearn to be by Heaven healed.

Our body is a friend indeed
Whose language we must learn to read
And listen, when its limits say,
"It's time to ponder, pause and pray."

Our stomachs told the need for food;
Our skin for warmth, when cold and nude;
Our brains for needful nightly rest:
When we obeyed, we rose up blest.

But as our youth becomes old age,
Our body turns another page
And bids our soul shake off its frown
To write the final chapter down:

Reviewing sights, retracing days,
Recounting gifts, repeating praise,
Repenting sins, reliving love,
Renewing hope in life above. . . .

Before our weary pen is still,
Rehearsing choices of our will:
What hands have clasped, where feet have trod,
How we believed or doubted God. . . .

And as our eyes grow dim and close,
Recalling what our body knows:
Despite good-byes in death's chagrin,
We'll rise to join this dust again.

– 1/8/2015

BABIES

All babies bring from heaven
Some vestiges at birth
To modify the burdens
And daily grind of earth.
Angelic light still gleaming
From eyes that know no guile,
They capture us with wonder
And charm us with their smile.

When parents are devoted,
Their inborn love protects
These precious little infants,
Just as the Lord expects.
But this is not the reason
He calls adults to share
Their sweet maternal nurture
And strong paternal care.

God sends us helpless babies,
So innocent and dear,
To challenge selfish habits
That we've picked up down here;
To lift us from our folly
And fill our empty cup;
To teach us precious lessons
And help us to grow up.

—10/5/2015

by David L. Hatton

EQUATIONS

Logic offers a realistic equation:

Free-Will Choice
(don't want to give that up)
   multiplied by
A Sense of Right and Wrong
(can't see tossing that either)
   equals
Moral Accountability
(must live with it, die with it)

But God offers a divine equation:

Our Moral Failures
(can't wiggle free of those)
   divided by
God's Grace in Christ's Cross
(if Jesus is Who He claimed)
   equals
Pardon and Peace for Eternity
(the result verifiable in real time)

Sound too good to balance out?

If God is truly a Lover
(as Jesus Christ portrayed Him),
Go figure! The latter equation is
the most human-friendly in existence!

I plugged my Free-Will Choice
into that divine calculation's Divisor.

Do the math yourself! It works!

              – 3/23/2014

Poems Between Here and Beyond

EVERLASTING

Though seas subside to plains of glass
And winds forget where they have blown,
Though centuries and eons flee,
Time cannot steal a thing from me:
Not one brief episode will pass
From all the moments I have known.

Though mountains proudly scratch the sky
With rocky fingers firm and fast,
Beside their rubble I will stand
And see them wither into sand.
I'll be alive to watch them die,
As they erode into the past.

While storm clouds drop their rain or snow
In winter's rush to circle round,
I'll mark the water's slow return
To restless salty waves that churn,
Until all rivers cease to flow,
As lakes and seas become dry ground.

When Earth was just a flaming ball,
The stars had twinkled ages long.
Yet when all galaxies are gone,
My fruitful soul will journey on.
My reach shall span beyond them all,
As their light wanes and mine grows strong.

Unless the Maker makes them true,
Such boasts as these are mad and vain;
But sharing His eternity
Is part of human destiny.
I bear His image. . . so do you:
All worlds must end, but we'll remain.

– 12/8/2015

by David L. Hatton

PREVENIENT GRACE

Though preached by priestly scholars
    or a damning demon's voice,
Begone, that fruitless doctrine
    of "a will without a choice"!
If God demands that wayward souls
    must heed what they have heard,
Then saying, "They're unable!"
    makes a folly of His Word.

While all are "dead in sins"
    and darkly bound in Satan's night,
The lost have no excuse, because
    God blesses each with light.
His Word pervades creation—
    speaking loudly, shining clear—
To shake each blinded conscience
    wide awake enough to hear!

And that's the crux, my brethren,
    caught by Calvinistic creed
To controvert God's mercy
    meant to meet Man's fallen need.
Christ seeks out every straying sheep
    and calls them to repent—
Their free response enabled
    by His grace prevenient.

On both the good and evil
    God makes rain and kindness fall
And by His "whosoever will..."
    invites us one and all.
With every heart's reply foreknown,
    God chose our destiny,
Because His love's elective grace
    predestined liberty.

The Hindus teach that choices seem
   but are illusion still.
Reductionists say chemicals
   determine human will.
And Islam's fatalistic god
   has never been "good news."
But Scripture's Sovereign Lord ordained
   each sinner's chance to choose.

– 1/23/2014

GRIEF

Grief is the stretch beyond the pain,
A long and bitter-sweet refrain.

I trace again a trail we walked,
A spot where we sat down and talked,
Or see a gift, a card, a note,
And each rehearses songs it wrote.

Reviewing portraits on the wall
Or treasured visits, I recall
The smiling image of your face:
These mem'ries I dare not erase. . . .

As on I press through flowers and weeds,
Such aching surges then recedes,
Like salty waves that ebb and flow,
Until I reach my turn to go.

Till we embrace again On High,
Grief is the stretch, the long good-bye.

– 12/4/2013

by David L. Hatton

CHOSEN

God chose me for salvation
Before the world began
Through foresight of my future place
Within His holy plan.
He sees with perfect vision
The choices in the span
Of lives awakened by the grace
He gives to every man.

Our Maker—never driven
By arbitrary thrill—
Takes pleasure in restoring sight
That Satan tried to kill.
By sovereign love He's given
To every blinded will
A gracious portion of His light
That we might choose Him still.

There is no place for bragging!
God's love has paved the way.
We only leave our lifeless tomb
Beneath His Spirit's sway.
God's help is never lagging—
"While it is called today"—
To rescue sinners from their doom,
If they His grace obey.

—5/23/2015

DEFENDING HEAVEN AND HELL

Neither heaven nor hell
 needs any further defense
 to free-willed minds than this:

Light's passionate marriage to Love
  forever celebrates
  the pursuit of truth, and
Love's absolute allegiance to Light
  persistently refutes
  any commitment to lies.

Both heaven and hell
  mercifully demonstrate
  God's eternal promotion
  of authenticity.
Both places validate
  the everlasting human duty
  to chose the goodness
  of Love and Light.

Therefore, both destinies
  glorify the grace of
  a holy and loving Creator.

– 1/20/2013

PUNCTUATION'S ERADICATION

Free verse is refreshing, when flowing clear,
articulated with as much painstaking skill
as polished pens render metered rhyme.
Who cares if tight constraints are set aside,
as long as word-craft paints its portraits well?

But, laxity creeps in, exalted as authentic style,
expressive down-sizing, fresh unconventionality.
This modern shift gradually slipped beyond
older verbal efforts at mind-embodiment.
Past poets, free-verse pioneers and masters—
Whitman, Dickinson, Sandburg, Eliot, Pound—

by David L. Hatton

labored long to transmit their hidden thoughts,
palpable pictures, worthy wants and warnings.
Skilled with everything available in the toolbox
of our written-language legacy, they wrote
with one poetic goal: communication.

Deeming innovation equal to improvement,
relaxation synonymous with freedom,
some promise this dispensing with punctuation
has intensified the quality, the purity of poetry:
"Unneeded husks. . . eliminate them altogether!
They're out of place, antique, passé, confusing,
environmentally cluttering a poem's word-beauty."

Yes, in exactly the same way goal posts, flags,
boundary lines, bells and distractive rules
ruin sports events, spoil each player's enjoyment.
How would emancipation from these play out?
Feet running, balls sailing; no fouls, no score?
Are we pretending to be having fun yet, folks,
with lines stretching out amalgamated vocabulary,
regardless of winning or losing the word game?
Then resounds a blown whistle, and modern poets,
shrugging in confusion or sneering in contempt,
fail to recognize or recall what that signal means.

Punctuation evolved and fittingly survived
to dissect verbal blobs into edible portions,
to lay iron tracks for long trains of thoughts,
circumventing unintentional ambiguity—
a liability often mistaken as a virtue in verse.

Banning those tools in the name of liberty
set up a new standard for modern conformity
and begged the avoided but inevitable question:

Have we reached forward or rolled backward
by shifting clarity's burden from poet-shoulders
to a reader's ability to decipher unpunctuated
mental streamlines of consciousness?

Weary of this new legalism, I ask the wary,
Is this game played better unmarked, unpaced?
Examine what's been avoided or tossed
to see if the one tool left ("start a new line")
has sold us gemmed progress or jaded regression.

As reactionary counter-revolutionary, I still use
commas to pause or segregate concepts;
question marks to indicate queries or rhetoric;
parentheses to echo parallel ideas or feelings,
and *em-dashes* before stating them differently;
elipses to allude to trailing or further thoughts;
apostrophes to clarify what's owned or missing;
colons before explanatory words and phrases;
semi-colons to merge concept-related series;
periods to decide and announce conclusion.

To punctuate or not to punctuate: it's a question
seriously unasked and mindfully unanswered now,
and spacesbetweenwordsmaynextbelaidtorest.
Will modern conformists rebel at realizing
they've championed liberation by substituting
the boring repetition of new-line redundancy
for a richly diverse and long-trusted armory,
tested in the trenches of meaning's refinement,
or keep sacrificing the old work of clarification
on this impoverishing altar of popular minimalism?

– 4/27/2016

by David L. Hatton

THE DISCUS THROWER

Machine-like man, possessed with concentration,
Propels a wheeling, smooth and level hop
To spring with skill from trained coordination
Across a ring, rotating like a top.

This discus thrower—sturdy, iron tower—
Extending mighty muscle-rippled arm,
Unwinds his body in one burst of power,
As with the hurl he roars a fierce alarm.

The once dead plate, enlivened by the cry,
Bolts, catapulted from his maddened hand
In frantic, climbing whirl to scrape the sky,
Till earth's pride pulls the saucer back to land.

The winner's disc will mark its distance thrown
To boast his form, release and muscle tone.

– 1964 (revised 4/16/2016)

MY MARRIED HEART

In all desires
And all intents
That love inspires
With age or sense,
These sweetest fires
Find this defense:
As strength retires,
They flame intense!

My married heart
Is merry still...
While passion's art
And wedded thrill—
Which at the start
Began to fill—
Now flood my heart
With all my will!

– 2/14/2013

QUESTIONS

What lasting satisfaction comes to him
Who seeks to satisfy his troubled soul
With transitory pleasures that grow dim
And seem to mock the joy that was his goal?

What gain is there in trying to repay
A gift unmerited, as if a debt?
Can grace be found to hold our guilt at bay
Until our gratitude is real, without regret?

Is there security upon this sphere,
Assurance to confirm tomorrow's break,
Or does death's swift and final blow draw near
To halt the projects we would undertake?

To answer these questions, pity the man
Who tries without God, for he never can.

– 1965 (revised 2015)

by David L. Hatton

WHAT LASTS

Many a saying, a quote, a quip
Rattle my mind on my earthly trip.
But one of them stands, rings true, holds fast:
"Only what's done for Jesus will last."

To me my mother this proverb taught.
She said it often—'twas quickly caught:
"There's only one life; 'twill soon be past,
And only what's done for Christ will last."

So hard and long the rowing can seem,
Or life may float like a merry dream.
Roll what you will. . . . When the die is cast,
It's your words and deeds for Christ that last.

You may plant seeds that refuse to grow,
Or fail to reap what you tried to sow.
Though hopes were high and your visions vast,
Your work for the Lord alone will last.

As I draw nearer my time to go,
I have to share what we all should know:
On these short journeys that pass so fast,
Only what's done for Jesus will last.

– 2/18/2014

THE LOVE OF GOD

There's a fear I have of judgment...
Not of standing at the throne
Of the One Who made the burden
Of a world in pain His own.
But I tremble at the prospect
Of the shame I'll have to face
For the times I failed the sinner
By not showing love and grace.

When the gracious Lord of glory
Chose to wear our fleshly frame,
Feeling sadness for our sorrows
As He healed the sick and lame,
He was never hard on sinners
Caught and bound in Satan's maze,
But upbraided the self-righteous
For their proud, conceited ways.

Are we better than the mockers
Spitting hatred on our Lord,
Who when stretched in crucifixion
Made His pardon their reward?
Are we blind to our investment
In the stripes upon His back
When our tongues lash out at others
For the holiness they lack?

How shortsighted is our vision
Of the Incarnation's cost:
Jesus came to seek and salvage
The creation we had lost.
On that cross His life was broken
To redeem what sin had marred,
And the proof—in resurrection—
Is His body, ever scarred.

by David L. Hatton

We must hope for transformation
In the straying souls we meet;
All become His holy temples,
When they seek His mercy-seat.
Never doubt that God is willing
To restore the vilest heart,
For Love tasted death to offer
Each lost life a brand new start.

– 6/19/2014

VENGEANCE

By vengeance is human depravity sealed,
Both quenching compassion and freezing the heart.
Its bitter cold flame is in anger revealed
From wounds darkly pierced by a devilish dart.

In planning the payback, we dream of the worst,
While demons keep fueling injustices done.
Revenge, once ignited by satanic thirst,
Must even the score, and then up it by one. . . .

But Christ from His Cross prays with wisdom divine:
"They acted in ignorance, Father, forgive."
And God replies graciously, "Vengeance is mine
To fully repay, if they choose not to live."

God's passionate zeal is why hell is so hot:
His love for the truth scorches lovers of lies.
Though wronged, the avenger—a sinner—should not
Usurp Heaven's role; he'll get burned, if he tries.

– 1/13/2014

GLORY

How media and masses make us move
To crown the next immortal they approve!
The rich and famous shine to steal the show!
But then the spotlight fades . . . before we know.

The same oblivion becomes the fate
Of every idol whom we celebrate.
Our latest heroes fall from favored grace,
As brighter starlights flash to win the race.

So, what is popularity and fame?
The superficial knowledge of a name?
The surface recognition of a face
That turns of time eventually erase?

In stark humility our Savior came
And never tried to win the world's acclaim
Or gain approval from the status quo
Or seek the praise of powers here below.

He counted other honors merely loss
Before the humble pathway of the Cross.
He set the highest standard for the soul:
To gain eternal glory as the goal.

Christ's single focus was the Father's will,
And His revered example renders nil
The shallow prize of brief celebrity
For us who hear and heed His "Follow Me!"

– 1/20/2014

by David L. Hatton

TERMINUS

Hourglass empty;
Measured cord cut;
Opportunities passed;
Possibilities exhausted;
Game over. . . .

End of discussion:
No more opinions;
All choices chosen;
Personal history frozen:
The last period
Forever terminating
The last sentence
In each autobiography
(Once partly private,
Hereafter an open book).

End of the trail,
Concluding all steps
Down all forks in the road
To finish the journey;
Point of no return;
The ticket's last stop;
End of the line
At the final destination,
Where earthly life stops
And afterlife begins.

Whether delight,
In reward and rejoicing,
Or disaster,
In retribution and regret:
Gate shut. . . .

– 8/28/2015

GENDER

XX or XY:
DNA will never lie!
But the fickle brain can form
Fibs that fight against the norm.

XY or XX:
The Creator's will for sex!
"Male and female" was His plan.
"She is woman," said the man.

XX or XY:
Let the hardware not defy
How the Maker meant to wed
Couples in the marriage bed.

XY or XX
Forms the union God expects,
Procreates the human race
By the conjugal embrace.

XX or XY:
Human babies hear the cry,
"It's a girl!" or "It's a boy!"
From parental shouts of joy!

XY or XX:
Louder than the birth defects!
Longer than a mismatched feel
God can touch to soothe or heal.

XX or XY:
On anatomy rely!
Body language makes the case
Rhetoric cannot erase.

– 2/12/2014

by David L. Hatton

INQUISITION

From its height of papal glory,
Rome still bears a stain:
Cruelties and tortures gory
Of believers slain;
Hung or flayed to die of bleeding,
Burned alive in prayer,
Slaughtered for their Scripture-reading,
All by "Peter's chair."

Had their protestation perished
Under fire and lash
Or their hope for freedoms cherished
Vanished in the ash,
We today would too be liable,
As that martyred host,
Just because we owned a Bible
Or made Christ our boast.

Roman faith, if it has merit,
Cringes at these tales.
Mass and Mary can't repair it;
Explanation fails.
But the popes who wrote this story
Pray without refrain
That those flames be purgatory
Where their souls remain.

– 4/13/2015

ETERNITY

When we've been there ten thousands years,
We'll see our trips were brief:
Love will have swallowed up all fears;
Joy will have banished grief.

Our journeys, long and labored through—
The pains that seemed to last—
Will shrink beneath our future view
Into a narrow past.

The depth and breadth of Kingdom peace
Will dwarf the former strife,
When death, disease, and wars will cease
Amid eternal life.

Creation's freedom from decay
At last will be secured,
And hell will quench the battle fray
The faithful have endured.

Our minds will thrive in flesh restored:
Renewed identity.
The loneliness that we abhorred?
Dissolved in ecstasy!

The destiny of time and space
Eternity will frame,
And on His Bride I AM will place
His everlasting name.

Forever we will serve in roles
That He designed us for,
And boring tasks that wearied souls
Will plague the saints no more.

by David L. Hatton

While eons stream and pass us by,
And others take their place,
Our lips will praise our Bridegroom King
For His amazing grace.

– 10/24/2015

SOUL SLEEP

For eighteen hundred years was taught
That only corpses went to graves,
That souls went on, awake in thought,
While bodies slept 'neath dust or waves.

I choose to keep the older creed
That says our flesh must rest from toil,
Awaiting, like the planted seed,
That Day of Rising from the soil.

If later teachers' words are right—
That souls must sleep before they rise—
Then when I hear that Trumpet bright,
I'll wake up and apologize.

But if they're wrong, then their mistake
Was known the moment that they died,
For even now they're wide awake
Repenting for what they denied.

I'd rather be aroused from sleep
To find that I was duped by lies
Than be awake in death to weep
Till God decides to dry my eyes.

– 3/12/2013

MY SISTER, MY SPOUSE

It's sweet to touch your lovely face
And hold your hand in mine.
I gather strength from your embrace
Or when our lips combine.

With every kiss, endearment grows
To lift and thrill my soul,
And married grace the stronger flows
As aging takes its toll.

It matters not how much the house
Decays through passing years,
Or what we gain or lose, my Spouse,
Amid our joys and tears.

But what's important is the love
That wed our hearts as one
To seek and worship God above
Through Jesus Christ, His Son.

– 2/14/2014

EDEN'S TABLE

I lived with nature, and nature cherished me.
The Maker meant for us to dance
    throughout eternity.
But I loved a wisdom nature didn't know.
She only knew Who gave her life
    and caused her form to grow.

by David L. Hatton

I too sought beauty, though beauty was my home.
In hot pursuit of pretty things,
    I left her side to roam.
But, in my searching, I lost my deeper sight.
As on I chased elusive dreams,
    I stumbled in the night.

And I liked eating, so nature held a feast
To strengthen me to serve and rule
    the fish and fowl and beast.
But I craved knowledge to please my hungry will
With moral freedom's deadly fruit,
    which plagues creation still.

Yet God loved humans, who strayed from Eden's path
To wander—body, soul, and mind—
    beneath redemptive wrath.
He set a Table with His own Beauty's Love,
Inviting our return to feed
    on Wisdom from above.

Life's Tree has furnished this Food of mystery,
Renourishing the wayward self
    back to its destiny.
Christ is the Nurture, restoring Eden's bliss:
His flesh and blood, the holy Meal
    that sinners mustn't miss.

– 5/9/2015

ORIGINAL SKIN

Of one blood we were fashioned
   and of one skin we'd be,
If Adam hadn't eaten
   from that forbidden tree.

Since God's first plan was holy,
   sin's aftermath was ill,
But interracial marriage
   reminds us of His will.

– 8/8/2014

OLD WEBS

A dazzling whisper of a bug,
With golden form and fragile wing,
Was captured by the sturdy hug
Of web abandoned by its sting.

Did spider die or simply leave
The trap it spun with lethal plan?
No matter... Watch skill's past receive
The prey for which the ploy began.

The insect fights with slender might
Against the tattered, worn array.
But deadly strands grip much too tight
To let its poor life break away.

And so, the woven nets of old—
From profit-hunters dead and gone—
Still capture hopeful lives untold
Who struggle on, their dreams unwon.

– 3/28/2015

by David L. Hatton

TEARS OF LOSS

"Stop the pain of parting!
Stay the sting of loss!"
Is the mourner's moaning
Underneath the cross. . . .

He Who asks its bearing
Understands the state
Of a heart that's breaking
Underneath the weight.

"In this world of weeping,"
Says the Crucified,
"All is in My keeping—
All the ones who've died.

"Death is not an ending
But the follow-through:
Here, all souls are growing;
There, that growth pursue."

Trust—while you are mourning—
Him Who paid the cost
For the full renewing
Of the world we've lost.

Keep your faith, believing
Till that coming Day,
When these tears of grieving
He will wipe away.

– 3/15/2015

WHEN PRIDE IS BROKEN

Strong hammers of zealous pride
pounding out their hostility in every age
forever dash themselves to pieces
on the timeless Anvil of God's Word.

But those who break pride with faith
by falling on Christ the Cornerstone
reap every human-friendly joy
our loving Creator ever planned!

Such faith feasts on ultimate realities,
While pride self-smashes into oblivion.

– 3/2/2015

THE BODY SPEAKS

How foolish are the doctrines
Despising flesh and skin,
    Suspecting lust
    Within the dust
That we are living in!

Our Maker is an Artist
Whose compositions speak.
    The body's word
    Is seldom heard,
Except by those who seek.

There's artwork in the body—
Divine incarnate speech—
    And open hearts
    Can hear the parts,
For there's a voice in each.

by David L. Hatton

The head is close to heaven,
Because the brain must be
    A likeness of
    The God of love
And creativity.

The eyes need light for vision
To see if tales are true,
    And faith is blind
    Till rays divine
Restore our sight anew.

The ears can weigh vibrations
As sweet or bitter sounds.
    They run in flight
    Or take delight,
When guiding truth abounds.

The mouth shows need for nurture
That self cannot supply,
    And lips call out
    To those about
With their connecting cry.

The arms enfold their lover;
The breasts embrace their fruit.
    And to His side
    God hugs the Bride
Who treasured His pursuit.

The hands extend the image
That human work must bear
    Of Him Who willed
    That we should build
His Kingdom everywhere.

Poems Between Here and Beyond

The pro-creative organs
Are matched to meet as mates
    And bring by birth
    New life on earth,
As Triune Love creates.

The legs and feet, so busy
To crawl and walk and run,
    Predict our trail
    Shall never fail
Beyond the setting sun.

– 8/10/2015

WORTH REPEATING

A poem bears rereading,
    when it has hit its mark
to strip away the fig leaves,
    or free the prisoned lark
to soar on wings of duty
    to meet the Maker's will,
or stand—when God inquires—
    to greet Him naked still.

A song will beg an encore,
    when it has struck a chord
that makes our heartstrings echo
    with rhythms from the Lord.
Its melody, succeeding
    to bring us wide awake,
accompanies our travels,
    whatever trails we take.

by David L. Hatton

The stories, myths or fables,
    and parables of old
are heard again with relish,
    if—when they first were told—
our hopes and dreams found courage,
    or peace removed our fears.
We'll always feel their magic
    repeated through the years.

A saying, quote or proverb,
    a movie, skit or play
will help as well tomorrow,
    if what it brings today
entrances us with vision,
    revealing greater goals,
casts light upon our journeys,
    and settles in our souls.

– 7/17/2015

JUDGMENT

There comes defining moments
for every wayward soul.
They strike notes in a heartbeat
that echo from the whole.

Their dark reverberations
put angel wings to flight,
attracting hell's attention
to add them to its night.

And moments come defining
the souls whose notes ring clear
as echoes from a heartbeat
resounding godly fear.

By Love that fear is conquered
to shut the devil's door
and draw them into heaven
for bliss forevermore.

The choices of a lifetime
condense and are distilled
to paint a living portrait
of what our souls have willed.

The proof is in the pudding;
the flavor in the wine.
All fruits will dress a table
demonic or divine.

– 3/2/2015

REMINISCENCES

Sometimes we can see them,
   as once they were of old,
Long before God took them
   to walk the streets of gold—
Long before the decades
   put wrinkles on each face,
Back when time was timeless
   and death seemed out of place.

We can often hear them,
   rehearsing songs they wrote—
Our emotions hanging
   on every word and note—
Sending us to places
   where former joys remain;
Bringing recollection
   of tales and tears of pain.

by David L. Hatton

Are we entertaining
   these memories alone,
Hearing just the echoes
   without the flesh and bone?
Or do friends departed
   reach out across the spheres,
Reminiscing with us
   until our final years?

– 7/12/2015

RETIRING FROM NURSING

I've hung up my stethoscope, turned in my scrubs,
I'm anxious no more about protocol flubs.
I'm done with procedures and taking report,
No longer obsessed about lawsuits in court.
I've stopped dropping orders; I'm closing my chart—
No more bedside strain from suppressing a fart.
I've quit being tempted to come to work sick.
At last I am safe from a stray needle-stick.
No more changing gowns made organically wet
Or gathering stories I want to forget.
I've halted my search to find things out-of-stock.
I'm quitting my game of a race with the clock.
No more blowing veins with repetitive pokes
Or torturing patients with bad puns and jokes.

But I will miss working alongside a staff
Who humored my humor by feigning their laugh.
I never felt lonely surrounded by gals
Who called themselves "guys" and were always great pals.
These girls were alert! On the night shift, I've seen
Them wide-eyed with courage (or was it caffeine?).
I've watched them restrain their annoyance all night

When caring for patients who sit on the light.
They stand out as models of Nightingale's dream,
Accepting assignments while wanting to scream.
Of teamwork and trust, from this coworking crew,
How much I have learned! But alas, I am through.
The years have sped by, and I've relished each one,
But I must "Abandon shift!" now, . . . I am done!

– 8/17/2015

COUNTING DELIVERIES
(a song for my L&D coworkers, sung to the tune of "Counting Sheep" in White Christmas, 1954)

When I'm retired and cannot sleep,
Some precious blessings are mine to keep,
Although I may weep
Counting deliv'ries.

When failing mem'ry becomes my lot,
I'll just recall all the fun I got
From getting so hot
Doing deliv'ries.

I'll dream about the pushing,
and I'll see a crowning head,
Then call the Doc and baby nurse,
before I break the bed. . . .

So, if you're working in L&D
And see a phantom from history,
Remember . . . it's me
Counting deliv'ries!

– 5/7/2015

by David L. Hatton

REUNION

Today we grieve the absent kiss;
Tomorrow mourn the face we miss.
The coming weeks and circling years
May never dry our deepest tears.

But God's own hand will wipe away
These sorrows, when that coming Day
Brings missing loved ones into view—
When severed ties are joined anew.

No longer will we feel the grief
Of lost embraces—all too brief—
But we will greet and hug once more
Those dear hearts who went on before. . . .

It isn't far and won't be long
Until we sing that welcome song
Of sweet reunion up above
With all the treasured souls we love.

– 11/05/2015

ONE FAMILY

No man is an island.
We're part of the main,
Each made by our Maker
For links in a chain—
Not meant to meander,
As if in a dream,
But just like a river,
To flow in a stream.

God's trumpet has sounded,
Announcing His grace,
Inviting with welcome
The whole human race
To march out together—
Redeemed heart and soul—
To govern creation:
Our destiny's goal.

God planned for a union
Of humanity
To sail as one vessel,
Instructed but free—
His Spirit the trade wind,
Our hands on the helm—
To reign in the cosmic
And spiritual realm.

This is no audacious
Or fanciful boast!
Just question the creatures
And heavenly host.
They groan in their longing
For one final thing:
To follow the family
Who followed the King.

– 10/6/2015

EVER-CIRCLING YEARS

Our noisy table brood has slipped away,
This roof, its rules and rituals outgrown. . . .
Yet we still light the wreath that waits the Day,
Content to celebrate as two alone.

by David L. Hatton

As Advent marks the end of every year,
So lately it has brought a final word
About dear friends who've quit their journey here,
Whose "Merry Christmas!" won't again be heard.

Despair makes hope and peace seem overdue
Within this weary world, so worry-worn.
But Advent shines its starlight ever new
And welcomes love divine to be reborn.

Grace greets our griefs with Advent's sacred call.
The wreath's four candles? We'll ignite them all!

– 12/11/2015

CAN I ONLY GUESS?

I'm male, so can I really know
or even learn what it's like
to be a woman?

We wrestle in our youth,
struggling to come of age—
amid confusing voices,
brittle traditions,
abusive histories,
political agendas—
into gender identity.

While growing up, always
my insides felt as much
part "Momma" as part "Daddy."
The language between my legs
tipped the balance.

My wife's body language
confirmed our separate gifts.
Twelve children later,
lessons crystallized forever
in my work of helping moms
deliver and nurse their young.
I observed them losing
exploitation's social lies
about never finding fulfillment
in gender-distinctive anatomy.

After myriads of such meetings,
witnessing intimate episodes
that nurtured without defining
feminine self-affirmation,
no . . . I stand forever stunned,
still too mesmerized to fathom
the mystery of womanhood.

– 2/24/2016

MATERNAL POWER

Although you make jokes
  about pregnancy's girth
That stretches mom's belly
  before she gives birth,
Don't mess with the might
  of her laboring love
That crushes your hand
  as her push comes to shove!

– 5/16/2016

by David L. Hatton

CARING

This world around us surges—
  duties vie
    for all our time,
    our energies,
    our care.
But greater Duty urges,
  "Don't pass by
    a hurting heart
    with burdens hard
    to bear!"

Routine is not our master,
  nor is fear,
    or vanity,
    or trivia,
    or show. . . .
Amid a day's disaster,
  let's live here
    to lighten loads
    and griefs, before
    we go.

– 2/23/2016

MENTAL FOG

Translucent, murky, crawling cloud
Thwarting recognition's gist—
Familiar visions wrapped in shroud,
Mystifying mental mist. . . .

– 3/30/2016

DOOM

On earth, he claimed that God is not;
In hell, he swears that God is cruel. . . .
Such reasoning is so much rot
Upon the lips of either fool.

In life, he rendered God no praise;
In death, he wails a ceaseless curse,
With no more wish to mend his ways
Than when they grew from bad to worse.

In freedom, self was on the throne;
In chains, free-thinking disappears.
His mind had ceased to be his own,
Once demon hosts became his peers.

In hope, he knew the chance to change;
Despair makes room for no remorse–
Regret can merely rearrange
The doubts he forged by willful force.

In light, life's gifts wooed his belief;
In darkness, flames of anger burn. . . .
If grace still offered him relief,
Would he from evil choices turn?

– 3/24/2015

GHOST OF A CHANCE

The ghost looked very human, not haunting,
crouching on the bench, so sad and angry.
When fears lifted, I went and sat there too.

by David L. Hatton

"Not fair!" he shrieked inaudibly. "Liars!
They promised rebirth to work off karma.
But here I am, same ME! Memories, sins,
all still here. . . no fresh start. That's not fair!"

Trying to comfort by patting his shoulder,
my hand felt nothing and jerked back.

"Damn religion! Damn gurus! It's not right. . . .
pestered by thirst with nothing to quench it,
hungry but unable to eat. I itch but can't scratch,
forever racked with regret, wounds still stinging
with no chance of revenge for unsettled scores.
Where's God in all this? It's just not fair!"

I wanted to speak, but a freezing-cold shadow
fell upon us from a dark, approaching shape,
faceless but for its twisted, gruesome grin.

"I can help," slithered from blood-dripping lips.
"I'll take you where revenge is food and drink,
where the very air you breathe is vengeance.
Touch my robe and we shall go there now."

But, as the ghost began to raise his arm to meet
this vile fiend's extended, hand-less member,
courage swelled up from within, and I shouted,
"No! There's healing! Don't go!
Resist him! He's the devourer of souls!"

Too late . . . . Both vanished as the limbs met,
and I was left on the bench weeping, sickened
by the putrid, reeking, lingering odor of hell.

– 4/19/2016

Poems Between Here and Beyond

A SADDLED HORSE

Afield and afar, with a fiery star
Beaming its light through the gloom of the night,
'Midst overgrown weed stood a well-groomed steed
With a tail of snow and her mane aglow.

But the silver sheen of her coat pristine
Was trumped by the sight of a saddle bright:
Its leather was new with a golden hew,
With alluring gleam that caused me to dream.

I remained aloof when she stamped her hoof,
For I knew this meant the young mare was sent
As a mount to ride thither far and wide—
Her rider would own an adventure throne.

My courage was slack to climb on her back,
So she stamped again, my spirit to win,
And her eyes shone red, as I shook my head,
For I did not know where she planned to go.

Would she have me sit with no bridle's bit
Or reins to control her free-ranging soul?
Through her offered thrill, I'd be in her will
Like a wide-eyed child on a journey wild!

She began to prance as I turned to glance
At the fence and farm, where I feared no harm,
Where I did my chores and laid up my stores,
Where I made my bed and was safely fed.

Then, reading my mind, the horse reared and whined
With a neighing cry, as if in reply
To my wish to stay, and galloped away. . . .
Recalling my choice, I weep and rejoice.

−1/28/2016

by David L. Hatton

JUST BECAUSE

If Heaven held no sure reward,
No afterlife applause,
I still would imitate my Lord
And serve Him . . . just because.

Because His parables are true,
I'd study all He said
And try to learn what I should do
To walk the way He led.

Because He lived a life of light
And taught the truth of God,
I'd try with all my moral might
To trace the trail He trod.

Because I've found the singing sweet,
I'd gather with the throng
Who kneel to worship at His feet,
And I would join their song.

If I succeed in doing right,
Although the task is tough,
And end up 'pleasing in His sight,'
For me, that is enough.

Yes, even though I'm mocked by some,
I'd keep His loving laws,
Content to have, when death has come,
No trophy . . . just because.

—2/4/2016

LOVE THAT LASTS

How forcefully was I misled
By foolish lines my culture fed
To me, while yet naive and young,
Short songs of *puppy love* unsung.

Insistently, they taught a norm:
All men will fall for face and form
And long with lust at curves and hips—
This lie was preached from many lips.

If beauty, body parts and shape
Are "pitfalls" we cannot escape,
It fancies God, who crafted skin,
"A Teaser" tempting us to sin!

Against such sacred social lies,
The Maker of our inner eyes
Ordained *relationship* to be
The crown of sexuality.

The lesson worldly wisdom lacks
Is that a sweeter realm attracts:
When youth and figure's charms are gone
And wrinkles come, true love lives on.

The Lord designed two souls to wed—
One flesh within a marriage bed—
To build a home and live their vow,
For love's a choice, both then and now.

And so, my dear and lovely spouse,
Still mistress of our aging house,
Fret not about the fads and fears
That trouble hopes, engender tears.

by David L. Hatton

The world's deceit can't touch the truth
That lasts beyond the bloom of youth.
Your beauty grows, as does my thrill
In loving you—it always will.

– 2/13/2016

GREEN DOLPHIN STREET - 1947

When seeing it on TV as a clueless pre-teen,
I came away thinking and believing:
"*I could marry anyone, and make it work.*"

A street and a ship shared the same name
in this epic film, the ship appearing thrice
and rescuing the movie's hero twice.

But what started on that street—
so typical of over-told tales of romance—
took the hero half-way round the world,
where, love-dreams blown apart forever,
he learned the truth: *love is a choice*.

Did I say *hero*? Many players in the plot
portrayed what Hollywood back then
rarely dared admit: *duty trumps romance*.
In three crucial scenes, all bore one witness:
true love chooses to do what's right.

I found it on VHS years later, and my teens,
who hated "those old black & white movies,"
were enthralled by what had early flourished
in my own young mind: *love is a choice*.

– 2/12/2016

THE WILL

No will is weak.
All souls are strong
To choose their choices, right or wrong.

While wayward wills
Know to obey,
They rhyme and reason it away.

Though minds be weak,
Emotions frail,
Some launch with them as chart and sail.

Yes, wisdom warns,
And tempests chide,
But wants and whims won't be denied.

When hearts are bent
To have their way,
Their faulty wishes lead astray.

You doubt this true?
Review the Book!
Beware what duped desire took!

Forbidden fruit
Is still in style,
Along with sin's guilt-ridden guile.

We think we're free,
But we are not.
That dream's a ploy in Satan's plot.

by David L. Hatton

No soul is safe—
Our foe is set
On keeping us his servants yet.

But human will
Is free alone
Beneath the reign of Heaven's throne.

– 2/6/2016

DISILLUSIONMENT

Trusted leadings, never given;
Long awaited gifts, not sent;
Failing works, where we have striven,
Feed our disillusionment.

How we crave fulfilled perceptions—
Gaze at baubles, reach to take—
Mesmerized by dear deceptions,
Crushed on finding our mistake!

Time is short; the hours fleeting. . . .
Dream-filled games can often steal
Opportunities for meeting
People, paths, and treasures real.

Providential disillusion
Strips deceitful paint and masks,
Saves life's choices from confusion,
Spares us for authentic tasks.

– 3/29/2016

CELLS

I think no tongue or pen can tell
The riddles latent in a cell,
Whose gems precisely intertwine
To boast such intricate design.
Protected by a membrane thin,
To keep its treasures safe within,
This city filled with factories
Produces life's complexities.
While superstitious books advance
That DNA evolved by chance,
Each ribosome and organelle
Declares a Mind behind the cell.

– 3/4/2016

COMMUNITY

Awakened to it from the womb
   And nurtured by it at the breast,
Dependent on it till the tomb,
   Our need beyond a cozy nest!
Of leaves and limbs, the mother tree:
Community! Community!

We learned from others, not alone—
   Our single self is not the rule!
Upon a high and haughty throne,
   A reigning soul will play the fool
By treating with audacity
Community! Community!

by David L. Hatton

We find it not in mirrored looks
   Or journals penned by our own hands.
It thrives from reading ancient books,
   Connecting us by global bands
To timeless waves of history:
Community! Community!

It twirls within our work and walk—
   An earning-spending form of dance.
It sings in chorus, lives in talk
   With those we meet by date or chance.
This deep and daily mystery?
Community! Community!

Life interwoven never roams
   As isolated, island deeds—
Our neighborhoods, our schools, our homes,
   All ties of labor, commerce, creeds,
Announce one human destiny:
Community! Community!

– 3/14/2016

WISDOM

In worlds of hurt
   and wounding random
Fools and sages
   may complain,
But wiser wisemen
   hold in tandem
Heaven's balm
   with fortune's pain.

– 3/10/2016

AUTUMN

Autumn, or as some say, Fall,
Seems to paint in sunset hues—
Yellows, oranges, scarlets—all
Echoing the cyclic news:
Summer's done! It's winter's call!

Leafy arbor garb is tossed
Down on dying grass and ground.
Summer's verdant vesture, lost;
By brisk thieving breezes found.
Morning sprays them all with frost.

Chirping ceases; feathers flee.
Autumn drives the beasts away
Into sleep or poverty,
To await another day
Springing forth with growth and glee.

– 2/8/2016

LE JOUR QUE J'AI NAGÉ NU

Je n'avais jamais pensé de nager nu,
jusqu'à ce qu'un jour mes yeux ont vu
une écolière
dans une rivière,
complètement de vêtements dépourvue.

Tout de suite, mes joues commençaient à rougir.
En tout cas, je me retournais pour partir.
(Pas assez rapide!)
Elle criait, "David!"
En souriant, elle m'y saluait à venir.

by David L. Hatton

Donc, toute à coup, je l'ai bien reconnue:
à mon école, fréquemment, je l'avais vue—
pas bonne amie,
mais assez jolie—
ses appels persistants me faisaient détenu. . . .

J'ai dit, "Je suis sans maillot de bain!"
En se moquant de moi, elle agitait sa main,
"Tu as ton peau!
Entre dans l'eau!"
Et alors, je soumettais à son souhait enfin.

Bien que parfois j'ai espéré à voir
une fille nue, quand elle remplissait mon espoir,
la honte m'évitait;
le péché me fuyait!
Quel plaisir plus sain que je pourrais vouloir!

— 2/7/2016

OMG, GMO!
– a visionary lament –

Where waves the amber grain, O Lord?
Too darkly dust-bowl winds obscure
Mirages of our days gone by. . . .
Such barrenness! Is it Your sword,
This endless famine we endure?
Creator, hear our mournful cry!

No judgment poured on hybrid skills!
You blessed those hopeful trials and toil.
But science wizards crafted seeds
Immune when poisoned potion kills
The life within surrounding soil.
We bought their harvests without weeds.

"Who owns the seeds shall rule the world,
Controlling Earth's economy!"
Subjecting all beneath their spell
Of latent dearth, their labs unfurled
An oversight of wizardry,
A devil's plot devised in hell!

One subtle, sterilizing gene,
Implanted to insure their sales,
Became a virus! How it spread!
Now nothing planted springs up green!
Their GMO seed even fails!
God, grant us grains that are not dead!

When Monarchs dwindled, disappeared,
Bereft of special staple need;
When we watched bees become extinct,
Our fate was sealed! Too late we feared
Monsanto's monstrous growth and greed,
To which our starving world is linked.

The children wail! Their parents weep!
No house is safe from hungry thief!
The wizards hide who left the path
That nature nurtured us to keep.
Restore green life! Lord, send relief
From our presumptive error's wrath!

– 3/16/2016

by David L. Hatton

SKINNY-DIPPING

Skinny-dipping's Heaven's will!
Skin's equipped to feel its thrill!
God our Maker taught us how
Nine long months! So, why not now?

– 3/25/2016

A BEST FRIEND

Fame and fortune fluctuate,
Falter, fizzle, end. . . .
Nothing can annihilate
Faith in one's best friend!

– 3/29/2016

THE WIPING CLOTH

When He was here, nude like a slave,
He stooped before His Bride:
Our feet He humbly wished to lave
To free our hearts from pride.

And on the cross, stripped bare again,
He shed His precious blood
To wash away the stains of sin
And cleanse us in its flood.

Ascended now to Beulah Land,
With cloth that bathed our feet
Held gently in His loving hand,
He must this task repeat. . . .

Sojourning here these earthly years,
We've gathered dust that clung.
For tired trails and trial's tears,
That cloth He's used and wrung.

And when the Bride at last arrives,
That laundered rag will be
The wiping cloth to dry our lives
From sorrow's mystery.

– 3/30/2016

GOD CONDEMNED

The yet-unanswered whys and wherefores
Confronting Heaven's ways and therefores
May fan a doubter's flamed frustration
To sentence God by condemnation.

Hear grieving Job for justice crying,
Or Psalmists swear to cease from trying!
Such discontent of Earth with Heaven
Infects life's bread like bitter leaven.

But just compare how these two vary—
The footstool and the Sanctuary:
Let light divine from holy treasures
Reveal our willful, wayward measures!

Omniscient Wisdom's word stays golden,
As partial-knowledge boasts embolden!
The Maker's Mind needs no updating,
While human thoughts keep vacillating!

by David L. Hatton

When justly weighed, contrasted soundly,
These differ even more profoundly:
Arraigned with misconstrued depiction,
God's banished by a sham conviction.

Immune to such blind, judging action,
Behold Almighty Love's reaction:
Complaints His open ears have taken
Without one straying sheep forsaken. . . .

– 3/23/2016

SKEPTICS

Most arguments with skeptics
Are mainly wastes of time. . . .
Despite how sound the logic,
They'll reason and they'll rhyme
With clever, trapping loopholes
Laid out for fools to spring,
Not seeking rules of virtue,
But doing their own thing.

Good questions have pat answers—
They've memorized them well
From unbelieving scholars
And voices haunting hell.
Wise words won't be convincing,
But met with trick and taunt,
For truth's not what they're after
But thinking how they want.

– 4/4/2016

Poems Between Here and Beyond

NATURE'S TOUCH

Inner healing is not always
  but occasionally
  unanticipated spiritual epiphany.

Yet more often, it comes
  incarnationally—down-to-earth;
  the touch of caring hands;
  the beauty of creative hands:
  a painting, sculpture, poem, song. . . .

Sometimes, souls mend
  through ecstatic rendezvous
  with varicolored verdancy,
  birdsong, carved landscape—
  meeting outflowing energy
  primordially latent in nature,
  still reverberating vitality
  from her Creator's hand,
  despite age-long stifling
  under curse and chronic abuse
  by willful, wayward stewards.

Confused, trembling, taunted,
  a tortured conscience
  awakens to hope,
  emerges from inner depths,
  daring to reach out
  for nature's touch. . . .

Mysterious wonder meets wound;
  divine design defeats dread;
  echoing grace greets emptiness. . .
  and hurting heart—healing just begun—
    finally looks up. . . .

– 4/9/2016

by David L. Hatton

DOMINION
(an allegory)

Willy Wonka scattered tickets;
   set a golden Date.
People prayed and sought with hope of
   getting through the Gate!

Briefly sweet, delicious Heaven's
   thrill soon waned. . . . Alas!
Even Charlie, sad, disheartened,
   felt its pleasure pass.

But Almighty Master Wonka,
   Candyman-Who-can,
to the faithful, saintly Charlie,
   prophesied His plan:

"Sharing My delights in Heaven?
   That was not my Goal!
My creation needed you to
   rule in full control."

Human Charlie willy-nilly
   grabbed some chocolate bars,
gripped the hand of Candy Maker,
   shot beyond the stars!

– 4/11/2016

SIN'S DOUBLY CAUSTIC
(double-acrostic)

Sin is when a person's life misse**s**
Its mark and makes marring graffit**i**
Not only without but also withi**n**.

– 5/25/2016

GRIEF'S RIPPLES

Just like an ordinary stone,
once glistening on a rock-filled shore,
by hand at random picked and thrown
into a lake and seen no more,
so death's whim seems to pick and toss
our loved ones into graves of loss.

How quickly sudden splashy plop
resounds just once within our ears;
the stone we watched before its drop
in one split second disappears—
abruptly ends the voice we knew
with face familiar lost from view.

But in the water where it sinks,
that rounded rock leaves ripple rings;
and just as grief relives, rethinks
a thousand dear remembered things,
so echoed waves of loving run
which help a healing never done.

– 5/10/2016

THAT UNBLINDING LIGHT

Merely for their mounting mass, I trust tales
most skeptics doubt about glimpses beyond.
Those travelers rued returning, coming back here.
Such stark luminosity, too bright for naked eyes,
was much too soothing a bath for naked souls.

by David L. Hatton

Yes, that otherwise blinding illumination,
emanating with vital, penetrating intensity,
unveiled all—from their swim in uterine seas
to hovering, hurled headlong out-of-body—
all events relived, their past refelt in a flash.

Then, as metal hyper-magnetically attracted,
their disembodied selves shot up irresistibly
speeding forth toward the irradiating Source:
not Light alone, but all-knowing Presence;
not sheer power, but Love's living Personality.

Forgotten, all shock or suffering at departure,
until that loving Being's dread telepathic word
ordaining reluctant reversal: "Not your time yet."
Jolted back to this dim, cramped pain and clutter,
can anyone blame the returnee's sworn regret?

– 5/2/2016

OVERDUE PUN

A pregnant mom, quite overdue,
   heard her big baby's plea:
"Hey, Mama, let me outta you!
   Dere's no more womb for me!"

The mother, quicker than a blink,
   responded with some wit:
"You'll soon head out, but don't you think
   that's stretching it a bit?"

– 4/15/2016

SHAKESPEARE'S PEN

Prolific and enlightening,
Shakespeare with his pen
Wrote plays replete with humanness,
Chastity and sin.

Simple saints and star-crossed lovers
Sanctified his page;
Careless kings and wanton witches
Strutted 'cross his stage.

Scenes with awkward situations
Laced his comedies;
Wise and eloquent orations
Graced his tragedies.

Scripts where honor fought ambition;
Love and duty churned;
Passion wrestled with contrition:
Crowds to these returned.

He wove lines in verse's measure—
Beauty wed to wit—
Wrapping tales the world would treasure,
Never to forget.

Curtains fall on poet-sages. . . .
Famous names will fade,
But the Bard has won the ages
Where his pen is played.

– 4/15/2016

by David L. Hatton

HEALP!

I was too sick
to cry out, 'HELP!'
Pain came so quick,
it made me yelp
to heaven, "HEALP!"
No time to pray,
'My Maker, HEAL!'
In my dismay
I sent a squeal,
just one word, "HEALP!"

"I know how deep
the trials gall,"
He said, "but KEEP
your faith! Don't fall
or fret. Just KNEELP!
If pains you feel
wreak havoc wild,
I won't say, 'KNEEL,'
my hurting child,
but simply, 'KNEELP.'"

— 5/4/2016

HOW GOD ANSWERS

We do not know how we should pray,
a verse in Scripture states,
but never fret about the way
this fact of faith relates:

If our request is not quite right
or wouldn't help us grow
or leads us off the path of light,
why then, He answers, "No."

Or, if He knows omnisciently
we're wrong about the date
we think He ought to hear our plea,
then He will answer, "Wait."

And if it's discipline we need,
while asking Him to bless
in ways that feed our lust and greed,
sometimes He answers, "Yes."

But guidance in petitions true
is free for anyone
who'll seek the Holy Spirit's view
and pray, "Thy will be done."

– 5/11/2016

MOTHER'S DAY

Many children love the touch
Of your soft caring hand.
They may not show their thanks enough,
However well they've planned.
Enthralled by your maternal care,
Ready for your embrace,
Siblings, coming home today,
Delight to kiss your face. . .
And so do I, your faithful mate,
Your sweet devotion celebrate!

– 5/8/2016

by David L. Hatton

DEAD RIVALS

You know, to my unmissed dismay,
One of my rivals dies each day.
They have a sudden heart attack,
Or accidentally break their neck,
Or suffer long before they die,
And though it's sad, I never cry.

When obit sections post the news,
I fail to weep or get the blues!
Is this the way I should behave?
No grief to see them meet the grave?

If you're like me, there's no dismay,
Although a rival dies each day.
Why let it go? Why just forget?
They're always ones I've never met!

– 4/18/2016

PRAYER LIST

I thought I'd check my list today
of those for whom I need to pray—
my family, my friends, my mate,
and all who face a fearful fate—
for praying's free and won't reduce
the store of grace it scatters loose.

Before I was an older chap,
I thought such lists a needless trap
that fostered guilt, if rushed or missed:
just one more legalistic twist
to burden spontaneity
in saintly quests for piety.

"Just let the Spirit lead!" I said,
and so He would, when I was led
to listen to His quiet voice.
But circumstance can hinder choice—
today my aging mind forgets
to pray petition's proper debts.

So prayer lists have become my tools,
not to be shunned as lifeless rules,
but memoranda for my brain,
a railroad track to guide my train
of supplication I should send
for mate and family and friend.

– 5/7/2016

INDIANA SEASONS

Icy, snowy winds die down
and turn to breezes fresh with life
that blow a warmth into the ground
whose hair was cut by winter's knife.

Broad white blankets disappear;
bare skeletons of wood turn green;
the flowered meadows reappear
to beautify an April scene.

Berries ripen in patches dense,
as summer breathes its hot, moist air.
Brief showers give a sudden rinse
to cool the green world everywhere.

by David L. Hatton

Winds pick up and chilly breeze
brings autumn's magic brush of frost
to paint the leaves of bush and trees
all red and yellow, orange and lost.

Winter hides the naked earth
again with fleecy quilts of snow,
which sneak away at spring's rebirth
until once more fall's last winds blow.

– 1966 (edited 5/20/2016)

BEGINNING GARB

When God had finished sculpting us,
He deemed it "good" to see us nude,
but once we'd sinned, we made a fuss
and labeled naked bodies "lewd!"

In shame and fear we hid in dress
with fig-leaf ingenuity—
such textiles merely raising stress
by fueling curiosity.

"Where are you now?" God queried first,
to stop us from our sinful flight,
and if we wish to miss the worst,
we'd better halt and answer right.

"Who said you're naked?" next He asked,
to blow the devil's tricky scheme,
and yet most keep their bodies masked,
while faithful nudists let them gleam!

– 5/11/2016

THE CHURCH BELL

The steeple chimes with its church-bell rhymes,
A wedding day to bless.
There's not a spot in the parking lot:
A healthy crowd, no less.

Will couples come when the echoes numb
From vows they hallowed there?
Each marriage needs what the pulpit feeds
With Heaven's loving care.

The church bell chimes with its merry rhymes,
A christening to cheer.
There's not a space in the parking place:
So many souls are here.

But who will go, as the children grow?
God wants His lambs to thrive:
Each home and brood need the Maker's food
For spirits to survive.

The sad bell tolls—with a dirge it rolls
On grieving hearts of friends.
It seems too loud for the tearful crowd,
As one more story ends.

That faithful bell has much too tell.
Its beckoning rings true
That all should seek God's face each week,
Until our journey's through.

– 2/11/2016

by David L. Hatton

FALSE POETRY

When words enfold clandestine thought
And lips conceal a hidden heart,
A rhythmic ruse is sometimes taught
To ears attuned to verbal art.

Arranged by practiced wit and skill,
A verse can reach into the mind
And grab the reins, for good or ill,
To guide or garble, loose or bind.

As painted lies may trick the gaze,
So poor but pleasant lines, when heard,
May lay a trap of moral maze
For minds to miss the higher Word.

With eloquence in days of old,
When seers sang false prophecy,
They captured simple souls with bold
Refrains enshrined in poetry.

Let all beware these phrases tooled
By wayward tongues with measures bright.
Prevent your will from being fooled:
Immerse yourself in psalms of Light.

– 4/18/2016

HELL'S HARVEST

The harvest of hellish hereafter
   is sure as the sowing of sin.
Its screams won't be louder than laughter
   resounding from demons within.

The skeptics who fled jurisdiction
   of conscience, commandment, and King
will find our "old myths" were nonfiction,
   while theirs had a poisonous sting.

Since tricks of the Tempter were treasured
   midst warnings of prophets grown hoarse,
regrets will unravel unmeasured,
   unchecked by eternal remorse.

While children of wisdom will flourish,
   rewarded for heavenly goals,
dark demonic armies will nourish
   their lust on hell's harvest of souls.

– 5/4/2016

FREE FALL

A poet tree
is hard to climb
for free-verse feet
that trample rhyme.
Yet, even worse,
on metered trips
of rhythmic verse,
their footing slips.

Tradition tried,
in years gone by,
not ways to hide
but clarify.
Its path of rules
for metaphors

by David L. Hatton

helped even fools
through verbal doors.

But freer trails
are traveled now.
Good grammar fails,
and poets bow
to whims which tell
a path of fate
where pens can't spell
or punctuate!

– 5/17/2016

OLD GLORY

With easel set not far away,
but far enough to miss its shade,
the pastel painter launched his day
to capture oaken glory's staid
and stolid, stalwart, sad display.

As contour sketch, laid steady down,
outlined the edges of the tree,
he felt a mesmerizing frown
cast from the trunk in mystery,
as from an ancient king's renown.

At once, the artist's tutored hand
seemed caught and taught in measured dance,
as pigment pure spread out unplanned
to paint the old oak's steadfast stance
beside the lake and forest land.

The limbs that dangled graybeard moss
took on an ageless majesty;
the gnarled bark, with purple gloss,
declared its royal sovereignty
midst summer's gain and winter's loss.

The painting draftsman's fervent skill
applied each otherworldly hue
as chosen by another's will—
"Impressionistic rendezvous!"
he muttered then, and says so still. . . .

– 5/1/2016

BREATH OF LIFE

Spirit life into dead dust
by Makers's breathing blown—
meant for higher living—must
explore a vast unknown.

Whether many days or few,
self's soul must journey free,
tasting love and sipping dew
in nature's symphony.

Reminiscent of the Wind
that blew the mind alive,
mysteries and marvels blend
for human hearts to thrive.

Awestruck by creation's voice
that echoes Heaven's will,
wisdom chooses to rejoice,
before breath's gift is still.

– 5/6/2016

by David L. Hatton

GREED

While avarice makes rich men poor,
the grateful poor are rich:
the attitudes that mold the core
of both determines which.

Unsatisfied with all its store,
the grasping fire of greed
burns hot to glut and gather more
beyond authentic need.

Contentment hangs among the keys
that open up the lock
to gracious golden treasuries
from which it shares its stock.

But lust can never quench its thirst;
its hunger reigns as lord;
its wealth is doomed, forever cursed
by hands that heap its hoard.

Let wisdom guide you not to take
this stingy path of gain;
in peace you'll sleep, renewed awake,
while greed grows more insane.

– 5/12/2016

WHY SO BIG AND OLD AND DARK?

At just the speed Big Bang exploded,
at proper weight of cosmic mass
and just the pull with which it's loaded,
a world for living came to pass.

Poems Between Here and Beyond

The rate of entropy's decaying
precisely at this cosmic stage
created circumstance for laying
an astro-brief anthropic age.

From core's death-dealing rays climactic
exactly far enough we stay
between two spiral arms galactic,
surviving in the Milky Way.

The Sun is at a perfect distance,
and when it throws a lethal flare,
Earth's strong magnetic-field resistance
protects our health with special care.

The timing and the right locations
of planetary real estate
set up two ideal situations:
we thrive and we investigate.

The solar system's lone location
with our transparent atmosphere
allows dark nightly observation
to make the cosmic story clear.

These fine-tuned facts in such alignment—
and I've shared just a few, you know—
seem placed on purpose by assignment,
as if a Planner willed them so.

On-target variables combining—
how fast the blast, how long stars burn,
our time and placement intertwining—
provide us space to live and learn.

by David L. Hatton

This vast array of such precision
seems not some fluke of happenstance
but meant to offer us a vision,
that we might seek our Maker's dance.

– 6/3/2016

EARTH, EARTH, EARTH

He Art, He Art, He Art, He Art—
before . . . behind our earthly start,
when, by His strong creative hand
that formed the sea and motherland,
He sculpted dust for lasting worth:
HeArt, HeArt made eArtH, eArtH, Earth.

His Heart, His Heart, His Heart, Heart, Heart,
seeking a world that fell apart—
pursuing souls who breathed His breath
to rescue them from realms of death,
re-image them by second birth:
His Heart, Heart, Heart for eartH, eartH, Earth.

Now Hear the Art . . . yes, Hear the Art,
Who sings—a course divine to chart—
inspiring Guide for human tales
with breezes blown to hoist our sails,
His wind instills artistic mirth:
O, Hear the Art call eArtH, earth, Earth!

Lost children of this groaning Earth,
return and find your pristine worth
as portraits of the Triune Love
in Father, Savior, Spirit Dove:
re-taste what Life and Light impart
from He Art, Heart, and Hear the Art!

– 6/28/2016

FLOWER TALK

You never have talked with a flower?
One whispered to me, as I dreamed;
she captured me fast in her power
with petals that glistened and gleamed.

She said she awaited the waking
of humans, asleep in their sin,
to destinies bright and breathtaking
that start from devotion within.

She chided our broken condition—
our wills running wayward and bent—
and told of our need for contrition,
returning with hearts that repent.

I felt that she somehow was reading
the doubts and suspicions I had
on hearing her sincerely pleading,
and my unbelief made her sad.

"We labor so briefly in beauty
but perish in cycles, until
you humans get back to your duty,
obeying your Creator's will.

"Fast bound in the curse you have brought us,
we still shine the light of His throne
in speeches the Maker has taught us
for making His majesty known.

"Don't shirk your responsible calling.
Behold how we wither and die,"
she moaned as her petals were falling.
"Our hope is in how you reply."

by David L. Hatton

Then silent, her last sentence spoken,
she drooped to the ground and was dead.
I woke, for the morning had broken,
and knelt on my knees by the bed.

Each time I now look at a flower,
I whisper a prayer to the Lord,
"Come quickly, O Christ, in Your power.
Make groaning creation restored."

– 5/17/2016

SEXUAL REMEMBERING

Remember the Creator,
Inventor of human sexuality,
Author of norms for its expression,
Maker of male and female bodies
explicitly equipped with special gifts
of gender-distinctive anatomy
for obvious reproductive function.

The great Designer's designation?
Life-long caring in conjugal vows:
a social home for procreative union,
not just for emotional wholeness
or physical safety from disease,
but a gender-balanced garden
for growing healthy new identities,
as long as wedded mates remember
to honor divine laws of love.

Addicted to spasmodic sexual thrill,
brains controlled by orgasmic spasm
could care less about self-integration;
trade mental reason for hormonal urge—
always wanting more, never satisfied,
forever hungry, running on empty—
and dismantle the meaning of persons
with dysfunctional seeds of social decay,
forgetting entirely how to remember. . . .

– 5/23/2016

"IN REMEMBRANCE OF ME"

They boasted nothing mattered
ten centuries from now,
"when history is scattered, . . .
forgotten anyhow."

Yet memories will linger—
when Earth has passed away—
on what the Maker's finger
carved into stone that day.

The truth divinely spoken
resounds eternally
against commandments broken
by pride's audacity.

But grace continues stable,
dispensed upon the poor
remembering the Table,
both now and evermore.

– 6/28/2016

by David L. Hatton

LABYRINTHINE JOURNEY

A forest meadow decked with hyacinth
Enfolds a brick-laid mystic labyrinth
Whose ancient Builder at its center set
A sundial wrought of bronze on marble plinth.

Step past its entrance. . . . You will not regret
The vast array of thoughts its paths beget
By twists and turns or steps of brief dead-end,
To pause, review, reflect, and not forget. . . .

Sometimes an unanticipated bend
Will lead so close to Center, yet will send
You out again to circumnavigate
Time's fringe, its long and lonely ways to wend.

At last, where maze of trail and dial mate,
Repose: a quiet space to contemplate
The gains and griefs that make life's labyrinth,
While outward days of will and choice await.

– 6/7/2016

Poems Between Here and Beyond

by David L. Hatton

ABOUT THE AUTHOR

David L. Hatton is an ordained Wesleyan minister with a BA in Bible from Maranatha Baptist Bible College (1972) and an MA in Cross-Cultural Studies from New College Berkeley (1988). Before becoming an RN in 1981, he served with Gospel Outreach in California and with Jeunesse en Mission (YWAM) in Quebec. He became a State-certified massage therapist shortly before retiring after 34 years of nursing (2015), having worked in the ER but spending his last 24 years helping moms deliver babies in L&D. David still pastors the small church of seniors he started in a retirement community in 1996. His hobbies are writing, art, and hiking with his wife Rosemary, with whom he lives in Sacramento, California. Married in 1971, they have 12 children and a growing number of grandchildren.

Poems Between Here and Beyond

by David L. Hatton

INDEX OF TITLES (alphabetical)

A SADDLED HORSE 78
A SHORT TRIP 32
ADELPHOR AND MORE 35
AFTERLIFE 12
AUTUMN 86
BABIES 40
BE OF GOOD CHEER 20
BEGINNING GARB 101
BEGINNING WISDOM 13
BLESSINGS 13
BODY LANGUAGE 39
BREATH OF LIFE 106
BREVITY 18
CALLINGS 19
CAN I ONLY GUESS? 73
CARING 75
CAUTION 24
CELLS 84
CHOSEN 45
CHRIST IS FIRST 16
CLOUDS 27
COMMUNITY 84
CONFESSION 21
COUNTING DELIVERIES 70
CREATORS 33
DEAD RIVALS 99
DEFENDING HEAVEN AND HELL 45
DISILLUSIONMENT 83
DOMINION 93
DOOM 76

EARTH, EARTH, EARTH	109
EASTER HOPE	32
EDEN'S TABLE	60
EQUATIONS	41
ETERNITY	58
EVER-CIRCLING YEARS	72
EVERLASTING	42
FALSE POETRY	103
FARTHER ON	24
FLOWER TALK	110
FREE FALL	104
GENDER	56
GHOST OF A CHANCE	76
GLORY	54
GOD CONDEMNED	90
GREED	107
GREEN DOLPHIN STREET – 1947	81
GRIEF	44
GRIEF'S RIPPLES	94
HEALP!	97
HELL'S HARVEST	103
HOW GOD ANSWERS	97
IMBECILITY	12
IN BETWEEN	11
"IN REMEMBRANCE OF ME"	112
INDIANA SEASONS	100
INQUISITION	57
JUDGMENT	67
JUST BECAUSE	79
LABYRINTHINE JOURNEY	113
LE JOUR QUE J'AI NAGÉ NU	86
LIFE'S TRAIN	25
LOVE THAT LASTS	80
MATERNAL POWER	74
MENTAL FOG	75

by David L. Hatton

MOM AND DAD'S 30TH ANNIVERSARY	23
MOTHER'S DAY	98
MY BEST FRIEND	89
MY DREAM OCEAN	14
MY MARRIED HEART	49
MY SISTER, MY SPOUSE	60
NATURE'S TOUCH	92
NO GRAY IN GOD	30
NOW AND THEN	22
OLD GLORY	105
OLD WEBS	62
OMG, GMO!	87
ONE FAMILY	71
ORIGINAL SKIN	62
OVERDUE PUN	95
PART OF THE CROWD	28
PLAGIARISTS	31
PLEASANTRIES AFTER MIDNIGHT	26
PRAYER LIST	99
PREVENIENT GRACE	43
PROTESTERS	14
PUNCTUATION'S ERADICATION	46
QUESTIONS	50
REDEEMING DEADLY SINS	18
REMINISCENCES	68
RETIRING FROM NURSING	69
REUNION	71
ROSEMARY	18
SEX VOW	16
SEXUAL REMEMBERING	111
SHAKESPEARE'S PEN	96
SIN'S DOUBLY CAUSTIC	93
SKEPTICS	91
SKINNY-DIPPING	89
SOLID	31

SOUL SLEEP	59
SOUND ADVICE	28
SUPERSTITION	17
TEARS OF LOSS	63
TERMINUS	55
THANKS SO MUCH!	15
THAT UNBLINDING LIGHT	94
THE BODY SPEAKS	64
THE CHURCH BELL	102
THE DEAD	26
THE DISCUS THROWER	49
THE INCARNATE GOD	34
THE LOVE OF GOD	52
THE WILL	82
THE WIND OF GOD	13
THE WIPING CLOTH	89
VENGEANCE	53
WEDDED GRATITUDE	23
WHAT LASTS	51
WHEN PRIDE IS BROKEN	64
WHY SO BIG AND OLD AND DARK?	107
WISDOM	85
WORD PLAY	34
WORTH REPEATING	66
WRITE!	19

Made in the USA
Lexington, KY
23 June 2017